# CONTENTS
1316.981

2012.101

ACCESS GRANTED

## SHADOW SQUADRON DOSSIER

### CROSS, RYAN

RANK: Lieutenant Commander
BRANCH: Navy Seal
PSYCH PROFILE: Cross is the team leader of Shadow Squadron. Control oriented and loyal, Cross insisted on hand-picking each member of his squad.

### WALKER, ALONSO

RANK: Chief Petty Officer
BRANCH: Navy Seal
PSYCH PROFILE: Walker is Shadow Squadron's second-in-command. His combat experience, skepticism, and distrustful nature make him a good counter-balance to Cross's leadership.

### YAMASHITA, KIMIYO

RANK: Lieutenant
BRANCH: Army Ranger
PSYCH PROFILE: The team's sniper is an expert marksman and a true stoic. It seems his emotions are as steady as his trigger finger.

# SHADOW
# SQUADRON

# SAND
# SPIDER

SHADOW
SQUADRON

# SAND SPIDER

WRITTEN BY
CARL BOWEN

ILLUSTRATED BY
WILSON TORTOSA

AND
BENNY FUENTES

2012.241

*AUTHORIZING*

Raintree is an imprint of Capstone Global Library
Limited, a company incorporated in England and
Wales having its registered office at 7 Pilgrim
Street, London, EC4V 6LB   Registered company
number: 6695582

www.raintreepublishers.co.uk
myorders@raintreepublishers.co.uk

First published by Stone Arch Books © 2015
First published in the United Kingdom in 2015

Designed by Brann Garvey

ISBN: 978-1-406 28571-0 (paperback)
19 18 17 16 15
10 9 8 7 6 5 4 3 2 1

British Library Cataloguing in Publication Data
A full catalogue record for this book is available
from the British Library.

Printed in China by Nordica
0414/CA21400598

## LANCASTER, MORGAN

RANK: Staff Sergeant
BRANCH: Air Force Combat Control
PSYCH PROFILE: The team's newest member is a tech expert who learns fast and has the ability to adapt to any combat situation.

## JANNATI, ARAM

RANK: Second Lieutenant
BRANCH: Army Ranger
PSYCH PROFILE: Jannati serves as the team's linguist. His sharp eyes serve him well as a spotter, and he's usually paired with Yamashita on overwatch.

PHOTO NOT AVAILABLE

## SHEPHERD, MARK

RANK: Lieutenant
BRANCH: Army (Green Beret)
PSYCH PROFILE: The heavy-weapons expert of the group, Shepherd's love of combat borders on unhealthy.

PHOTO NOT AVAILABLE

# CLASSIFIED

## MISSION BRIEFING

### OPERATION

**SAND SPIDER** 5678

I've received an urgent call from a senator involved with Shadow Squadron's budget. To say he has a request is not entirely accurate -- it's more like a demand. In any event, if we want to keep receiving funding for the team, we have to head to Mali and rescue his kidnapped son.

I expect the team's cooperation to be top-notch after the extensive cohesion training we've undergone with our new combat controller, Morgan Lancaster.

- Lieutenant Commander Ryan Cross

3245.98 ● ● ●

MALI

## PRIMARY OBJECTIVE(S)

- Determine location of hostage

- Escort hostage to safety

## SECONDARY OBJECTIVE(S)

- Avoid conflict with local forces

1932.789

0412.981

1624.054

## INTEL

*DECRYPTING*

# 12345

## COM CHATTER

- BRIEFING: information presented before a mission that is relevant to said mission

- COHESION: training required to help team members work together more effectively

- OPERATIVE: a secret agent or spy

3245.98 ● ● ●

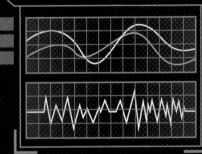

# COHESION

Lieutenant Commander Ryan Cross assembled his men in the briefing room as early as he dared, considering the previous evening's festivities. They'd held a going-away party for USAF Staff Sergeant Edgar Brighton, the team's former combat controller. The young soldier had been a member of the team since its creation, but he'd accepted a reassignment offer after a recent mission. From now on, he'd work for a highly classified psy-ops and cyber warfare division of the Department of Defense that promised to make better use of his intellect and technical skills.

That left Commander Cross with a hole to fill on his team. A rather big one, since Brighton was excellent at his job. But after a long period of paperwork evaluations and a handful of interviews, Cross was finally ready to introduce Brighton's replacement to the rest of the team.

That team was Shadow Squadron — a top-secret special missions unit. Assembled by the United States' Joint Special Operations Command, the unit was comprised of elite soldiers from all branches of the military. The team had soldiers from the Navy SEALs, Green Berets, Army Rangers, and the Marine Special Operations Regiment. They travelled all over the world rooting out terrorist threats, hunting international criminals, rescuing hostages, defending foreign leaders, and even fighting pirates. From one end of the world to the other, the team had showed up wherever the US government required military intervention but couldn't act openly for tactical, political, or legal reasons.

Cross's second-in-command was Chief Petty Officer Alonso Walker, a Navy SEAL like Cross. As usual, Walker arrived first, followed closely by the five remaining soldiers of Cross's team. Except for Sergeant Mark Shepherd, a Green Beret, none of them looked the worse for wear from their partying the night before. Shepherd was sporting a black eye from his ride on a mechanical bull at Brighton's going-away party. All of them sat quietly and glanced at the empty chair at the middle of the table. Brighton's absence was sorely felt.

"Let's get started," Cross said. He clicked on a computer touchpad built into the tabletop. The projector in the ceiling displayed the globe-and-crossed-swords emblem of Joint Special Operations Command on the computer whiteboard behind him. "With Staff Sergeant Brighton having moved on, we need to train his replacement and get the team back up to full cohesion."

The men nodded. When Shadow Squadron was created, the men had to go through nearly a year of special cohesion training. The purpose was to blend a group of individuals with different skills and military backgrounds into a functioning, singular unit. When Second Lieutenant Aram Jannati arrived from the Marines Special Operations Regiment to replace the

deceased Larssen, another month and a half of the same training was required to integrate him into the team. Now with the arrival of Brighton's replacement, another period of more cohesion training lay ahead of them.

Sergeant Shepherd spoke up first. "So who's the new guy? And when's he getting here?"

Cross grinned. "Now," he said. He tapped a button next to the touchpad on the table, keying an intercom. "Send Lancaster in," he said in the intercom microphone's direction.

"Sir," came the reply from a nearby speaker.

All the men turned in expectation as the door opened and the newest member of Shadow Squadron entered the room.

"Gentlemen," Cross said, "this is Staff Sergeant Morgan Lancaster, US Air Force Combat Controller."

"Morning," Sergeant Lancaster said. She closed the door behind her and waited. For what seemed like a long time, no one spoke or moved. Cross waited to see how his men would react to his choice.

As he'd privately hoped, it was Shepherd who broke the silence.

"A girl," Shepherd said. He stood up and crossed over to stand in front of her. The top of Lancaster's head came up level with Shepherd's Adam's apple, so when he stopped she had to look up at him. "I thought you'd be, um . . . prettier."

Anger flashed in Chief Walker's face. He leaned forward and opened his mouth to say something, but Cross stopped him with a glance and a subtle wave of his hand. Walker remained silent despite his obvious frustration.

"I beg your pardon?" Lancaster said to Shepherd.

"You know, like if you have to distract a guard with your pretty smile," Shepherd went on, as if what he was saying was completely reasonable. "Or if you have to infiltrate a high class society function in a fancy evening dress. You look way too tough to do any of that, if you ask me."

Lancaster let a hint of a smile play around the corner of her mouth. "Hello, Mark. It's good to see you haven't changed at all."

Shepherd dropped the act and broke out in a huge grin. He put out a hand and Lancaster shook it. "Hey, Morgan," he said. "It's been a long time. How's your sister doing?"

"Better off," Lancaster said. Her grin was bigger than Shepherd's now.

Walker relaxed a little. "So you two know each other," he said.

"Yeah, Chief," Shepherd said over his shoulder. "We went to high school together. I dated her sister." He turned back to Lancaster. "Still in the Air Force, huh? How mad are your folks about that?"

Lancaster shrugged. "They're mostly over it," she said. "Mostly, they just shake their heads in disappointment whenever someone asks if I joined the Navy like they did. This probably isn't the time to get into it, though."

"Yeah, fair enough," Shepherd said. He looked at Cross and saw the growing impatience on the Lieutenant Commander's face. "Sorry about that, Commander. Just caught me a little off guard, is all."

"No harm done," Cross said. To Lancaster he said, "Welcome, Sergeant. Have a seat."

"Thank you, Sir," Lancaster said.

To bring the team up to speed, Cross laid out a brief overview of Staff Sergeant Lancaster's background and qualifications. According to his research and interviews, Lancaster had joined the Air Force just before the Pentagon had removed the ban on women serving in combat roles in the US military. The ban had been an official Department of Defense rule since only the mid-1990s despite being an ongoing military tradition long before that. But with the most recent wars in Iraq and Afghanistan, women in supposedly non-combat roles were being put in exactly the same danger as their male fellow-soldiers. After a time, it became clear just how senseless and sexist the rule had been.

When the Secretary of Defense finally lifted the restriction, Lancaster was among the first wave of women who sought to push even further into the male-only special operations sector. While most of the military engaged in endless debates and bureaucratic foot-dragging, the Air Force's Combat Control quietly opened its admissions to women who were willing to meet its program's high physical and mental standards. Lancaster had been one of the select few women who made it all the way from the Combat Control Selection Course to Combat Control School. In short order, she earned her level-three ranking as a combat controller.

Afterwards, Lancaster was ushered through the Special Tactics Advanced Skills Training courses. She quickly learned free-fall parachuting and combat diving, among other specialized skills. Throughout the process, she earned some of the best scores and ratings in the past decade. Some of her scores were even better than Brighton's had been.

Cross described Lancaster's recent deployments and the medals she had won for her exemplary service. What he left out, however, was a revelation Lancaster had made in her last interview: being part of his team was not her ideal career move. Were it up to her, she would have continued her training until she became the Air Force's first female officer — not just an operative.

*In other words, she wants my job,* Cross immediately realized. And he couldn't blame her for her frustration. As progressive as the Air Force had been thus far, Lancaster found her progress stifled. The process of selection at the Special Tactics Officer level was a series of interviews with older, long-serving officers. Sadly, none of them had shown the slightest interest in considering her for the officer programme. While it was easier for the Air Force to move forward with integrating its male and female combatants, expecting the same progressive attitude from every individual was a dream yet to be realized.

All the same, Lancaster gladly accepted Cross's offer to join the team. Her sense of duty, Cross had come to realize, was greater than her specific career aspirations. The team needed her exceptional skills and dedication. And after all, Shadow Squadron did valuable work outside the cumbersome restrictions of the greater military bureaucracy. To Cross, it didn't matter whether that work was done by a man or woman as long as the soldier in question was skilled enough to get the job done. Lancaster was that sort of soldier, Cross believed.

"Welcome to Shadow Squadron, Sergeant," Cross said after he wrapped up the brief career and training history for the others.

"Hoo-rah," the men said in unison, echoing the sentiment.

Lancaster nodded, looking far more relaxed than she had when she'd first entered. She took her seat, and Cross began to lay out the extensive cohesion training to come.

* * *

Shepherd, Walker, and Cross were the last to leave the briefing room when the meeting was over. The soldiers had the next couple of hours to themselves, and Lancaster had been dismissed down to Supply to get her new equipment and speak to the tailor about her Shadow Squadron uniform. The standard Air Force uniform she'd worn in the field had been cut for a male body and didn't fit her quite right. One of the benefits of being part of Shadow Squadron was having a distinct field uniform that was also specifically tailored to each individual.

Shepherd was lingering by the door. "Say,

Commander, Chief?" he said to Walker and Cross. "Can I ask you something about Morgan?"

"Speak your mind, Sergeant," Cross said.

"Did you know we knew each other?" Shepherd said. "Me and Morgan."

"We didn't know about you and her sister," Walker answered. He'd helped Cross narrow his candidate selection to replace Brighton down to three. After that, he recommended Lancaster above the other two applicants. "I saw you went to the same high school at the same time, though. As small as your graduating class was, it seemed likely you'd met at least."

"That doesn't have anything to do with why you picked her, does it?" Shepherd asked. "Did you think that maybe since I knew her that'd make it easier for the other guys to accept her?"

"The thought crossed my mind," Walker admitted.

"Well, do me a favour, Chief," Shepherd said. "Don't tell her that."

"Don't worry, Sergeant," Cross said. "This team

doesn't need a kid sister or a mascot. It needs a good soldier who can do the work. Lancaster's proven to the Chief and me that she's legit, and I'm fully confident she can prove the same to you and the others on her own. Without your help."

Shepherd nodded. "Good. I'm glad to hear you say that, Sir," he said. "Lord knows I already have enough sisters of my own to worry about back home."

Walker frowned. "I'm willing to bet your sisters worry about you even more," he said.

Shepherd paused. "Fair enough," he said with a nod.

## INTEL

*DECRYPTING*
IIIIIIIII   IIIIIIIIIIIIIIIIII

12345

## COM CHATTER

- DRONE: an unmanned aircraft or ship that can be navigated by remote control
- RANSOM: money paid to a kidnapper or hostage-taker for the safe release of said hostage
- SURVEILLANCE: a watch kept over a person, especially over a suspect

3245.98 ● ● ●

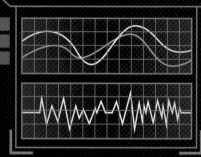

# CHAPTER TWO

# INTERRUPTION

Two weeks into Shadow Squadron's cohesion training, Cross called an unexpected meeting in the briefing room. He saw confusion on every face as the team filed in — even Chief Walker's. Cross couldn't tell if they could read his own aggravation and frustration in his features, but he hoped not.

"Change of plans," he said when everyone was seated. Fortunately, he didn't add "gentlemen" this time, which he'd been doing for most of the past two weeks whenever he addressed the group. *Little victories,* he thought. "We've got a priority mission that puts cohesion training on hold for now. Word just came through this morning. From high up."

"How high?" Chief Walker asked. "Command tends to give us our space during training."

"True," Cross said. He took a deep breath to stifle a frustrated sigh. "But Command's hands are tied on this one. By the purse strings."

"Oh," Walker said, reading between the lines. Lieutenant Kimiyo Yamashita, an Army Ranger and the team's sniper, nodded knowingly as well. The others looked confused.

"I've been on the phone half the night with Senator Jason Barron," Cross explained. "For those of you who don't know, he's the head of the sub-committee that controls our little program's secret budget." With that, all remaining confusion vanished from around the table.

"Yesterday afternoon," Cross said, "Senator Barron received this voicemail."

Cross tapped the touchpad on the table. Instantly, a scratchy and static-garbled voice came from the room's speakers.

## CLICK.

"Dad, it's Jack . . . Temedt office in Tessalit . . . have to help . . . I told them about my trust fund . . . by wire in one week . . . bad connection . . . week."

"That's it?" Walker asked after the recording ended.

"It's all the Senator's technicians could make out," Cross said.

"It's authentic?" Walked asked.

"Senator Barron is sure it's his son's voice, but the original recording is even worse than this one. It tracks, though. His son's been in Mali — which is where the city of Tessalit is — since he graduated from college. He's been working with this Temedt group in an effort to raise awareness of slavery over there."

"So Barron's worried something's happened to his son?" Staff Sergeant Adam Paxton asked.

Chief Walker nodded. "He probably doesn't like the sound of 'have to help,'" he said.

"That's exactly it," Cross said. "The Senator doesn't know any details, but he believes his son is in some sort of danger. Specifically, he's convinced himself that Jack's been kidnapped. Likely by some group of slavers the local Temedt office has gone up against. Jack has a trust fund set up by his grandfather, and Senator Barron believes the fact that his son mentioned it indicates there's a ransom demand involved here."

"But he isn't certain," Yamashita said flatly.

"Right," Cross said. "Neither the son nor any alleged kidnappers have been back in contact with him since. So they came to us."

"So what's the Senator want from us?" Shepherd asked.

"He wants our boots on the ground," Cross said. "We're to get into Mali, find and rescue his son, and bring him back home."

"Assuming he's been kidnapped," Paxton said.

"Assuming he's even still alive," Yamashita added.

"Right," Cross said again, his voice grim. "Should that not be the case, we're to 'find, root out, and punish the evildoers.' The Senator's words, not mine."

"Why us?" Paxton asked.

"Fair question," Cross said. "As the Senator explains it, no other team has the proper motivation to see this done as well and quickly as we do."

Cross saw his expression of distaste mirrored in the faces around the table. Yamashita broke the silence that had fallen.

"Meaning that Senator Barron is prepared to hold our budget hostage so we'll do what he wants," Yamashita said. "Ironic."

"Yeah," Cross said. "Very ironic."

"To think I voted for that guy," Lancaster muttered.

Walker looked up at Lancaster. For a moment, Cross expected him to growl a warning at Lancaster the way he always had whenever Brighton used to make smart remarks. Instead, the Chief burst out laughing. The others joined in as well, trading surprised looks around the table. Even Yamashita chuckled, which was a rarity all on its own. Lancaster scratched the back of her neck self-consciously and looked up at Cross with an apologetic shrug.

"All right, all right," Cross said. "Settle down. We have a trip and a blind operation to plan. And if the Senator's deductions are accurate, we've got less than a week to pull this thing off."

As the laughter died off and professionalism kicked in, Cross activated the table's touchpad once again. The overhead projector whirred to life. A world map appeared on the whiteboard, and Cross walked over to it. He touched a light stylus to Mali up in the northwest of Africa. Another tap broke the Mali map into its eight administrative regions, and Cross selected one of the two regions in the eastern portion.

"This is the Kidal Region," he said, centering it on the display. "In 2011, Tuareg and Islamist rebels tried to turn the entire northern half of Mali, including Kidal, into an independent region called Azawad. The Malian government was losing ground there, but then began taking it back by degrees with the French military's aid. Meanwhile, the Tuaregs have been fighting the Islamists as the Islamists have been trying to lay down sharia law in the region. US forces have been on the sidelines monitoring the Islamists for any connections that might arise to Al-Qaeda or other terrorist groups."

Lancaster nodded at that last part. She'd most recently been stationed across the eastern border in Niger as part of that effort, as well as to lend occasional aid to French forces active in Mali.

"Long story short," Cross continued, "it's a mess over there. The local armies on both sides of the conflict are a shambles, and law enforcement is iffy at best. And the farther north you go, the deeper you get into the desert, which means communities are smaller and farther apart. Very Wild West. Slavery is an issue as well. It's against local law, but it also has a strong historical and traditional backbone. Organizations like this Temedt group that the Senator's son mentioned are doing what they can to combat it, but the farther you get from solid government control, the harder it is to wipe out."

Cross touched his stylus to the whiteboard once more, indicating the western half of Kidal. "This district in the middle of the mess is Tessalit Cercle," he said.

Cross tapped again, narrowing down the scope of the display further. "This is Tessalit itself, the rural commune at the centre of the district. Most of the greater area is either desert plains or part of the Adrar des Ifoghas mountain range; the commune is at an oasis in the mountains. This is Jack Barron's last known location. According to his own social media updates, he moved out there from Timbuktu last June. Our intelligence suggests that the mountain badlands of Adrar des Ifoghas are home to scattered camps of rebels fleeing Malian and French forces."

Cross took a breath and paused before continuing the briefing. The next part would be a tricky aspect of the mission, and he wanted to make sure he emphasized this next part. "If there are slaver groups operating in the area, they could be hiding there just as well," he said. "We'll start our investigation here and borrow some recon time from satellite flyovers and the drones we have on station in Niger to help us keep an eye over the mountains. Command's already arranging for the satellite time. Lancaster, you'll be on point arranging the drone surveillance."

"Sir," Lancaster said.

"There's not much else to say at this point that we can't go over in flight," Cross said. "This is a blind operation with a tight deadline. We'll have more information on local contacts and a full aerial recon picture by the time we arrive. After that, all we can do is wait and see and react. So get your gear. We've got an hour before our first flight takes off."

## INTEL

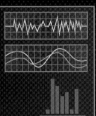

*DECRYPTING*
||||||||||| |||||||||||||||||||

### 12345

## COM CHATTER

- CV-22B OSPREY: an American
  tiltrotor aircraft capable of vertical
  landings and ascents
- FAMAS BULLPUP: a French-made
  assault rifle capable of fully
  automatic fire
- M1161 GROWLER: a durable but
  lightweight military vehicle designed
  to be transported by Osprey aircraft

3245.98 ● ● ●

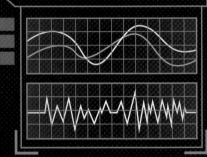

# OUTREACH

In no time at all, the team gathered its gear and boarded two of its state-of-the-art CV-22B Ospreys for the long trip to Mali. The Osprey could take off and land like a standard aeroplane or vertically like a helicopter. With its extended range and additional wing fuel tanks, the Osprey was able to cross the Atlantic and make it all the way to Africa in one uninterrupted flight, slowing only for in-flight refuelling.

That's not to say the ride was a particularly comfortable one. The flight crew, half of Shadow Squadron, and half the team's gear filled much of each Osprey. In addition, each cargo compartment carried an M1161 Growler. The vehicle was a light utility, light strike, fast attack model much like a Jeep, but slimmer and with less armour. With so much space in use, standing room was at a premium. It was all the soldiers could do to get up and stretch their limbs during the long, monotonous voyage.

Shadow Squadron actually touched ground first in Niger after a fast flyover of Mali. The trip added their planes' own forward-looking infrared radar imagery to the growing cache of aerial reconnaissance Cross and Lancaster had arranged for. The Ospreys set down at the small airfield that Lancaster had helped set up when she'd been assigned there by the Air Force. A handful of technicians crawled over the aircraft like ants to check for signs of wear and tear after the long flight. They also removed the modular extra fuel tanks, refuelled the regular tanks, and spot-checked the formidable armaments. By the time the checkup was finished, the Ospreys had been subtly transformed from long-haul workhorses to sleek, short-range birds of prey. The team then climbed back in to head west into Mali.

"You didn't want to catch up with your old pals?" Shepherd asked Lancaster once their Osprey was airborne again. The combat controller had spent most of the brief layover fiddling with the special gear she'd packed for the trip. "You were stationed here, right?"

"That was almost two years ago," Lancaster said. "All the guys I worked with have rotated out to other assignments. Besides, what could I even tell them about my new job?"

Cross overheard that and nodded grimly to himself. It was a hard fact of military life that the more elite and specialized a soldier became, the harder it became to relate to those soldiers outside one's immediate team or others at the same level of specialization. And it didn't get more specialized than the black-level secrecy under which Shadow Squadron operated. Lancaster didn't seem especially troubled by what she said, merely a little wistful, but Cross made a mental note to bring up the topic after cohesion training.

In no time at all, the Ospreys touched down at a

raggedy, all-but-deserted airstrip on the fringe of the Tessalit commune. When the Growlers were unloaded and Shadow Squadron had divided its personnel and gear into them, Cross gave the Osprey pilots their orders and led the expedition into Tessalit. The first stop would be the local Temedt office. Cross had been unable to make any sort of contact with the office by phone while en route. He hoped an in-person visit would prove more fruitful.

The office, when they finally found it, was nothing to write home about. It was a plain, brown, and square stone building that looked just like the ones to either side and across the street. Inside, a teenage girl doggedly pedalled a stationary bike connected by belts to the ceiling fans that did nothing to cool the air but at least kept it circulating. She spoke neither English nor French, but Chief Walker spoke in Bambara and learned that the head of operations was in his office at the rear of the building.

The head of operations made no secret that he was not pleased to see soldiers in his office, but he told Cross what he wanted to know. Jack Barron and his partner, a local man named Pierre Sanogo, were on a charity outreach mission in a distant village named Cadran Solaire. The Temedt officer was surprised that Barron might have been kidnapped, claiming he'd heard nothing of the sort. Barron hadn't checked in yet this week, but he wasn't expected back in Tessalit before Saturday. The Temedt officer offered to arrange a place for Cross and his soldiers to stay if they wanted to wait until then, but Cross declined. All Cross wanted was a location, directions, and local maps to compare against his own. When he got those, the team set out again.

An hour later, the Growlers pulled into Cadran Solaire. It was a modest collection of small, square, single-story stone buildings nestled into the crook of a sandstone valley with a single narrow pass on the far side. In one corner of the valley lay a deep, still pond of fresh water. A crooked spear of wind-smoothed stone rose out from the water as tall as a pine tree. Twelve round, flat rocks had been placed around the edge of the pond in a circle, each carved with Roman numerals representing the hours of the day. It was easily the biggest sundial Cross had ever seen.

A gang of some dozen children played soccer in the dusty street. As Shadow Squadron pulled in, they all stopped to stare, blocking the Growlers' path. They crowded around the vehicles, chattering excitedly in Bambara, speaking to the soldiers as if they expected them to understand their language. Cross had no idea what they were saying, but he did catch a few words: Légion étrangère in French. He cut his Growler's engine and signalled for Chief Walker to do the same. They stepped out, leaving their vehicles where they stood.

"We're looking for Jack Barron," Cross told the assembled crowd in heavily accented French. "Or maybe Pierre Sanogo. They're from Temedt."

Walker repeated the question in Bambara. As the name penetrated the crowd, a chill seemed to settle on the kids. They became strangely reserved and took hold of the soldiers' hands to pull them toward the village.

The procession filed into the village past a few wary-looking adults standing in front of their homes in the shade of makeshift awnings. A man in a loose, sleeveless robe met them halfway. He greeted them politely enough but asked them bluntly why they'd come. When Walker told the man who they were looking for, the man backed off without a word and let the children continue leading the way.

When the kids finally gave way, they were at a building near the narrow canyon that led out of the far side of the village. A Jeep larger and heavier than Shadow Squadron's Growlers sat parked outside it. The Jeep had a heavy machine gun mounted on the back. Two men in Malian army uniforms without rank or company insignia lounged against the Jeep, chatting in low tones. When Cross and then Walker tried to ask who the men were, the children either pretended ignorance or acted as if they didn't see anyone. They were adamant that Barron and Sanogo were inside the building, however, so Cross and Walker thanked them and sent them back off to play. The kids merely retreated to a safe distance to see what would happen next.

"Chief, with me," Cross said, nodding toward the building. "Everybody else, keep an eye out."

With Walker behind him, Cross went in to find Jack Barron. The building was someone's home, he found. A low table, washbasin, and clay oven dominated the main area. A sleeping area lay sectioned off behind a ratty cotton curtain. Seated at the table in the main room was a hard, muscular man in plain fatigues like those on the men by the Jeep. A FAMAS bullpup rifle stood leaning against the table in arm's reach. Across from him sat a local man in civilian clothes and a foreigner who could only be Jack Barron.

Barron looked quite different from the clean-shaven college kid in his father's reference photos. Gone were the polo shirt and chinos and the sixty-dollar haircut. Now he wore a faded cloth shirt over khaki cargo pants. His sun-bleached hair hung down past his ears in limp, disordered curls. His skin had been baked earthenware brown everywhere except around his eyes and in two bars over his ears. The skin there was still mushroom-stalk white from his overprotective eyewear. His arms were skinny like a monkey's and his long-fingered hands couldn't seem to stay at rest, even in the moment of surprise when

Cross and Walker entered.

"Jack Barron?" Cross said, pointedly ignoring the other men. "US military. Got a minute?"

"Aww, man," Barron groaned. "My dad sent you, didn't he?"

## INTEL

\*DECRYPTING\*
|||||:|| ||:||||||:|||

12345

## COM CHATTER

- GREEN BERET: special forces (soldiers) from the US Army

- M4 CARBINE: a lightweight and compact assault rifle capable of fully automatic fire

- SLAVER: a dealer or trader of slaves or slave labour

3245.98 ● ● ●

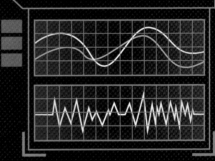

# CHAPTER FOUR

# ALTERCATION

"Well, clearly I haven't been kidnapped," Barron said, as if he were explaining things to an idiot. "Didn't my father tell you?"

Cross, Walker, and Barron had stepped out of the house and were huddled off to one side speaking in low tones. Barron's partner, Pierre Sanogo, and the man in fatigues remained inside to continue their business. Jannati and Yamashita waited by the door of the house while the rest of Shadow Squadron milled about waiting for orders. Shepherd seemed to be locked in a staring contest with one of the men guarding the armed Jeep.

"Your father wasn't very clear on your condition," Cross said through his teeth. "He neglected to tell us he spoke to you after that voicemail you sent him."

"Weird," Barron said. "Why would he do that?"

"I'd love to know," Cross said. "What did you two talk about?"

"Work," Barron said, maybe too quickly. "And my trust fund. Mostly that."

"What about it?" Walker asked. Cross remembered that Barron had mentioned the trust fund in his voicemail as well.

"I was trying to get Dad to give me some money out of it," Barron said. "My grandfather's will makes him the trustee, but I'm supposed to be able to decide how the money gets spent. Until I turn 25, though, I can't get any money without my dad's approval."

"What did you want it for?" Walker asked.

"Work," Barron said quickly, breaking eye contact. "You know, work-related stuff."

"Let me guess," Cross said. "You want to donate it to Temedt."

"Yeah," Barron said. "You know, for the cause and all that."

"But he wouldn't okay it?" Cross asked. Barron shook his head. Cross added, "And what happened when he told you that? I imagine you argued."

"More than that," Barron said. "I told him I was going to call my lawyer. If my cell phone hadn't died, I would have done it right then. As it is, I'll have to wait 'til Saturday when Pierre and I are back in Tessalit."

"You're not going to have to wait," Cross said. "We've got a sat-phone. Once I get off line with Command, you, me, and your father are going to have a little talk. Chief, keep an eye on him."

Cross stalked away to make the call to Command, leaving Walker and Barron alone. While he waited for the computer to recognize his voice and access code, he listened to Walker and Barron talk.

"I don't get this," Barron was saying. "Is your captain ticked at me?"

"He's not a captain," Walker said. "And it's not

you. If there's anybody who's going to get an earful, it's your father. He pulled some pretty important strings to send us racing over here to rescue you from trouble he knew you weren't actually in. Senator or no, your father's going to have to answer for that."

*You got that right,* Cross thought. He kept his voice relatively calm and professional when he got his Command contact on the line, but he insisted that Command conference in the Senator without delay. He smiled grimly when the Command operator put him on hold to contact Senator Barron's office.

Before he could get the Senator on the line, a commotion demanded his attention and he had to hang up. Shouts in English, French, and Bambara erupted from the house where they'd found Barron. One of the voices belonged to Lieutenant Jannati, whom Cross had sent to keep an eye on things by the door. When Cross looked over, neither Yamashita nor Jannati were where he'd left them, and the other members of his team were stirring themselves to confused action by the door.

Cross had taken no more than a step in that

direction himself when the man who'd been meeting with Barron and Sanogo staggered backward out the door and fell on his backside in the dusty street. Jannati emerged a second later and kicked the man in the back as he tried to roll away. Yamashita and Pierre Sanogo came out next. Sanogo looked horrified and reached out to pull Jannati back from the man on the ground, but Yamashita stopped Sanogo with a firm hand in the centre of his chest. The sniper's eyes scanned from Jannati to the man on the ground and then over to the Jeep the man had arrived in. He cocked an eyebrow at what he saw, then looked over at Shepherd.

Cross then saw what the sniper had seen. The two men who'd been guarding the Jeep were scrambling into action, hurriedly yanking the FAMAS rifles slung over their shoulders into their hands. Fortunately, Paxton and Shepherd saw the same thing. Stepping apart, they raised their M4 carbines and barked sharp orders for the two men to stand down. Hospital Corpsman Second Class Kyle Williams followed suit when he saw what the two Green Berets were doing. Lancaster hesitated, looking from Jannati to Cross

and then back to the two FAMAS-armed men before raising her weapon. The two Jeep guards stopped and pointed their rifles at the dirt, glancing at each other uncertainly.

Jannati drove another kick into the downed but still squirming man's ribs. The Malian yelped but remained on his knees.

"Lieutenant!" Cross yelled at Jannati. "Stand down, soldier!"

Jannati backed away just slightly out of kicking range, but his face was still a mask of rage.

Chief Walker ordered the two Jeep guards in Bambara to drop their weapons. He held his weapon across his chest and stood in front of Jack Barron, shielding him in case bullets started flying.

Finding themselves outgunned, the Jeep guards lay down their weapons and then backed off. Shepherd looked at Lancaster and nodded toward the weapons. She gathered them up and carried them over to Cross.

Cross stalked toward Jannati and stopped

opposite the man Jannati had kicked. "Explain yourself," Cross said firmly.

"Let this one explain it," Jannati said, throwing an accusatory glare at Pierre Sanogo. He gave a second one to Barron. "Or maybe the fortunate son over there."

"I said explain yourself," Cross growled, staring Jannati in the eye.

Jannati gritted his teeth, but Cross could tell the Marine wasn't angry with him. Jannati took a deep breath to compose himself, but the look of outrage returned when he glanced at the Malian at his feet.

"I overheard this piece of work talking in there while you and the Senator's kid were outside," Jannati began. "He's a slaver thug. He was trying to extort money from Temedt to leave this village alone. He's running a protection racket."

Although he wasn't as worked up as Jannati, Yamashita nodded his confirmation with a cold, faraway look in his eyes.

Cross heard Barron suck in a horrified breath.

Sanogo looked similarly stricken, but he only hung his head, the shame in his eyes failing to deny the accusation. Neither man looked surprised by Jannati's revelation but rather dismayed that the secret had come out in front of other people.

"So you just decided to go cowboy justice on him?" Cross demanded. "This isn't why we're here, Lieutenant."

Jannati couldn't have looked more surprised if Cross had slapped him. "Sir, I—"

"Quiet! I don't care what this two-bit lowlife's up to. He's not the mission." Cross pointed at Barron, who flinched as if Cross had pointed a weapon at him. "He's the mission. And frankly, I'm getting to the point where I don't care what happens to him, either."

Barron gulped. Jannati winced. Cross pressed on.

"Now take Mister Sanogo back in the house," he said. He made a gesture taking in Jannati and Yamashita. "I want the pair of you to keep an eye on him, but keep your hands to yourself. You read me?"

"Sir," Yamashita said. Jannati said the same, though it took him a few seconds to compose himself enough to say so.

"And you," Cross said in French to the Malian half-crouched in the dirt. "You understand me? Get up."

The Malian did so, glaring at Cross with plain hatred. Blood oozed from a swollen lip, and he clutched his side with one arm, breathing heavily. Bruised ribs, probably. "I don't care who you are or what you're doing here," Cross told the man. "Get your men, get in your Jeep, and get lost. I don't want to see you again before we fly out of here."

The Malian's eyes narrowed but he nodded. He hobbled over to his comrades, who looked just as helpless and defeated as he did.

"Sergeant," Cross said to Lancaster without taking his eyes off the wounded Malian. "Go make sure there's nothing else in their Jeep that we don't want there."

Lancaster tilted her head at the odd way Cross had worded the order. She paused for a moment but

then nodded and did as told. She left the two FAMAS rifles on the ground near Cross. When she reached the Jeep, Cross called out to the three Malians in French again.

"Hey, look at me," he called. "We're keeping these guns. I'm sure you've got more back home, but I strongly suggest you don't bring them back here."

The Malians grumbled and frowned at that but were in no position to protest. When Lancaster finished with their vehicle, she backed off to let the Malians clamber into it. They piled in and peeled out, tearing off through the sandstone canyon in a cloud of dust. Cross looked around to make sure his people were all right. He noticed that all of the locals had scattered into hiding. *Probably for the best,* Cross thought.

"What did you just do?" Barron asked in a scared, small voice. "You have no idea who that is."

"Let me guess," Cross replied, "that's why you actually wanted your trust fund. Protection money."

"Not that it matters now," Barron moaned.

"You told your father as much?" Cross continued.

"I tried to explain how things work over here," Barron said, "but he just said, 'You don't negotiate with these people, son. It only emboldens them.'"

"He's got a point," Cross said. "The more money you give people like that, the more they're going to want. Eventually they're going to bleed you dry if you don't stand up to them."

"That's easy for you to say," Barron said. "You don't live here. Plus, you've got the Army behind you. What do these people have? Not much against that guy you just humiliated in front of all of them. Do you know who he even is? His name's Bubaga, but the locals call him the Spider. He's not just some slave broker. He runs guns to the Islamists and the Tuaregs all over Azawad. He does protection rackets and human trafficking over three regions. He's got an entire army he formed from rebel deserters and mercenaries the government couldn't afford to pay anymore. Bubaga is a dangerous man, but for all that, he's at least honourable. He respects money, and I've got more than plenty to spare. I could've handled this if you hadn't interfered."

"Except you don't have that money," Cross said. "Your father wouldn't sign off on it, right? If you told him what you're doing here and who you're dealing with, that's probably why he sent us out here. He didn't want you to have to deal with Bubaga when you couldn't deliver the money you promised."

"I could've explained things," Barron said, though without confidence.

"Unlikely," Walker said, returning. He looked at Cross and said, "Ospreys are on the way, Sir."

"What's an Osprey?" Barron asked.

"It's our ride," Cross said. "And yours too, if you want it."

"What? You're just . . . leaving?"

"Yep," Cross said. "Full of sound and fury. As far as I'm concerned, this mission's over. You're accounted for and free, so my team's done. You're welcome to fly out with us, of course, but you're not obligated. You're a grown man."

"Bubaga is coming back here, you know," Barron said. "You understand that, right? He's going to wait until he sees you leave, then he's going to come back with his men to take out what you did to him on these people. Don't you think you have a responsibility to deal with that? Especially since one of yours caused the problem in the first place?"

"What I think is that I'm getting my people in the air when our ride gets here," Cross said. "You can go with us or you can stay here. Choice is yours."

"Fine then!" Barron spat. "Go! But I'm not abandoning these people. You can go home if you want, but good luck explaining to my father what you're letting happen."

Cross turned away without a word, signaling to Walker. The two of them walked away to gather up the men, collect the Growlers, and wait for the Ospreys to take them away from Cadran Solaire.

## INTEL

*DECRYPTING*

12345

### COM CHATTER

- .50 CAL: a heavy-duty bullet used in larger machine guns
- AMBUSH: the act of lying concealed in order to surprise an enemy
- OVERWATCH: a small unit that helps observe the battlefield
- TRACKER: a device that tracks the location of something or someone

3245.98 ● ● ●

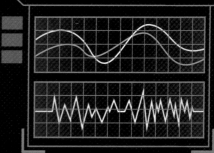

# ADAPTATION

The team's Ospreys traversed the darkening Malian sky. "Speak your mind, Lieutenant," Cross said to Jannati, who hadn't said a word since the Ospreys had arrived in Cadran Solaire. Also on his Osprey were Lancaster and Yamashita. The other Osprey carried Walker, Shepherd, Paxton and Williams. Lancaster sat hunched over her laptop computer, the glow from the screen illuminating her face.

"We can't just leave them there, Commander," Jannati said. He was no longer scowling or frowning, but he still didn't look happy. "Those people have no idea what this guy is going to do to them."

"I agree completely, Lieutenant," Cross said. He'd spent the first several minutes of the flight getting back in touch with Command to request any available intelligence on this Bubaga character Jannati had pummelled and humiliated. The file Command had sent back read like something out of a comic book villain's biography. Bubaga's wartime atrocities were almost as bad as the crimes Bubaga's own criminal gang had wrought against the civilians who defied him.

"That's why we're not leaving," Cross said.

Jannati blinked. "I beg your pardon, Sir?"

"If we were just turning tail and going home, we could've driven the Growlers back to the air field," Cross explained. "Bringing the Ospreys in and dusting off like we did was all for show. I wanted Bubaga to see us leaving and think the village is undefended."

"You're sure he was watching?" Jannati asked dubiously.

"Lancaster?" Cross said, looking at the combat controller.

"His Jeep stopped about half a mile outside Cadran Solaire and waited there until we'd lifted off and were out of sight," Lancaster said, looking up from her laptop. "He took up his original heading after that. I'll let you know when he stops again."

Jannati looked at Lancaster, clearly confused.

"I put a tracker on his car when I was pretending to search it for weapons," Lancaster told him. "Well, I searched it too. But I also placed the tracker."

Cross was pleased Lancaster had read his implied instructions without needing them spelled out.

"So we're going back to the village?" Jannati asked, relieved.

"No," Cross said. "We're going to assume this guy's coming back there as soon as he gets to his hideout, rearms, and gathers his men. We're going to set down in his path and intercept him. If we do this right, the villagers shouldn't be aware of what's going on until it's already over."

Cross rose and activated the high-definition teleconference screen mounted on the wall. On it appeared a cargo-bay view of the other Osprey as seen from the perspective of its own teleconference screen. Walker was visible on-screen, and the other three soldiers with him were gathered around him.

"We're ready here, Sir," the Chief said. "Do we know where the target's headed yet?"

Cross looked at Lancaster. She swiped something from her laptop's touch-sensitive screen toward the Osprey's teleconference screen. A digital contour map of local terrain appeared on half of the screen. A blinking dot labelled with a radio frequency ID appeared, moving through a narrow path through the mountain. The dot represented the tracker Lancaster had hidden on Bubaga's car.

"The path he's on dead-ends into that mountain," Lancaster said. "I don't see any signs of a base, though. My best guess from available aerial recon is that it leads into a cave system or just a complex where he's settled his slaving network."

"Or a *web*," Walker said. "You know, because he's called the Spider." Cross stared blankly at Walker. "Sorry, Commander. Go ahead."

Cross finally allowed himself to grin. The Chief must miss Brighton — now he was the one chiming in with bad jokes.

"Anyway," Cross said. "I'm not keen to chase this guy and his mercenary thugs down into unfamiliar caves in the dead of night. Instead, we'll meet him halfway when he sets out for Cadran Solaire's blood."

Cross dragged his fingertips along the half of the teleconference screen showing the digital aerial map, moving the image backward along the path Bubaga's Jeep had taken.

"Here," he said. The part of the road he'd indicated cut a blind curve through a sandstone pass with a steep wall on the inner curve. There was a sharp, shorter embankment on the outer side. "Chief, you got it?"

Walker tapped his screen, making a blip appear on Cross's screen. "Got it."

"This is where we'll hit them. We'll park one of the Growlers here." Cross tapped the screen, leaving a bright dot on the map. "This'll be Attack One. If we can blow part of this rock wall down to block the road when they get there, that would be ideal. Lancaster, you and the Chief will assess the terrain."

"Sir," Walker and Lancaster replied.

"I want the other Growler here. This is Attack Two." He tapped the screen again. "If not, we'll have to put Attack Two here." One final tap. "Right around this blind curve where they won't see it until it's too late. I'm going to need a volunteer to man that gun."

"Yo," Shepherd said, raising his hand.

"It's yours, Sergeant," Cross told him with a grateful nod. Shepherd hadn't chosen the easy job. If Attack Two had to pull double-duty as a roadblock, it was going to be terribly exposed. Cross turned to Yamashita and indicated another area on the map that was near the ambush site. "Lieutenant, I was thinking here for overwatch. Is this close enough?"

"What's the scale on this map?" Yamashita asked.

"Oops, sorry," Lancaster said. She tapped a few keys on her laptop, and a scale measurement appeared in the bottom corner of the screen.

Yamashita peered at the screen. "It'll do."

"Good. Lancaster, once you set the explosives — or don't — you'll take Four-Eyes and go with Yamashita. You'll keep in constant contact with the Ospreys as well, on the off-chance we need their firepower for support. I don't want you down in the soup on this one, though."

"Sir?" Lancaster asked, looking insulted or deeply disappointed.

"I'm not being chivalrous, Sergeant," Cross told her. "You haven't finished cohesion training with us yet. Until you do, you're on overwatch."

"Oh," Lancaster said with a quick nod. "Sir."

"Paxton, set up here at Cover One," Cross went on, indicating another section of the map, this one behind the ambush point. "If they try to run and get past us, you're the goalie."

"Sir."

"Williams, Cover Two's going to be here. Our gunners are going to be the most exposed when the shooting starts, so I want you to be where you can get to them fast. You've also got a partially covered route out to Cover One if Paxton's hit."

"Sir," the corpsman responded.

"Jannati, you'll be on the gun at Attack One."

"Hoo-rah," Jannati said, his eyes dancing.

"Chief, you and I will drive the Growlers into position and support the gunners."

"Sounds good," Walker said.

Without another word, Cross turned to go and give orders to the Ospreys' flight crews. Before he closed the cabin door behind him, he heard Lancaster turn and speak to Yamashita.

* * *

The sun had set when Bubaga's men set out for their intended retaliation against Cadran Solaire. The new moon sky glowed with a dusting of countless stars, and the sound of engines carried for miles through the darkness.

"They're coming, Commander," Lancaster said through her canalphone. From her vantage at overwatch, Lancaster was watching the road through the camera of the remote-controlled "Four-Eyes" quad-copter that Edgar Brighton had built.

Cross lay in the dirt at Attack One a few yards away from the Growler manned by Aram Jannati. His M4 carbine was propped on his half-empty backpack. His AN/PSQ-20 nightvision lens painted the ambush point in shades of bright green. "How many?" Cross asked.

"Five full Jeeps, one man each on the .50 cals," Lancaster reported. "There's an ACMAT truck behind them. It has a large cage on the back."

"Is it empty?" Cross asked.

"Yessir."

"Noted," Cross said. "Seems Bubaga intends to bring any survivors back to his base as slaves."

"That ACMAT could work to block the road behind the Jeeps," Yamashita said over the channel.

"Make it happen when we drop the roadblock in front," Cross said. "Cover One, move to Cover Two."

"Sir," Paxton replied. A moment later, he reported that he was at his new position.

Another few minutes after that, Lancaster reported that the Jeeps were right around the corner. Cross ordered his soldiers to get ready. The engine noise was right on top of them, and the Jeeps' headlights shone from around the blind corner. Cross lifted his nightvision lens so the headlights wouldn't blind him. "Contact. Roadblock ready."

"Ready, Sir," Lancaster said.

The first Jeep's headlights passed right under the high sandstone shelf where Cross and Jannati's Growler was perched. No one in the Jeep seemed to notice them waiting up there. Nor did they spot Attack Two ahead. Two more Jeeps rounded the corner. Then two more. The ACMAT came last.

"Close the road," Cross said.

"Sir," Lancaster said.

Cross looked away as the C4 plastic explosives exploded ahead of the Jeeps. The night shook with a heavy boom. Rocks the size of barrels tumbled into the road. A cloud of dust billowed out in all directions.

A second later, a muted crack sounded at the rear of the slaver convoy. Cross saw the windscreen of the ACMAT shatter inward as Yamashita eliminated the driver with a silenced shot from his M110 sniper rifle. The truck nosed toward the edge of the road and coasted to a stop, blocking the way out. The five Jeeps were now trapped between it and the rockslide.

"Attack One, Attack Two," Cross said. "Go."

## RAT–TAT–TAT–TAT–TAT!

## RAT–TAT–TAT–TAT–TAT!

Jannati and Shepherd opened up with the Growler's guns, cutting into the first and last vehicles in the line. Jannati targeted the ACMAT's hood with a laser-accurate stream of 7.62x55mm NATO rounds from the minigun, blowing the engine to smithereens so no one could drive away. From farther up, Shepherd sprayed a second stream into the lead Jeep. The driver of that vehicle slammed on his brakes as Shepherd's bullets tore into the side of the vehicle and sent gouts of black smoke pouring from under its bonnet.

The Jeeps left in the middle lurched to a stop, and the men within reacted in a semi-coordinated panic. The second one backed up a few feet and made as if to try to manoeuver around the smoking hulk of the first Jeep. Its headlights washed directly over Attack Two, illuminating Shepherd at the M134 and Walker in a shooter's crouch behind a rock. The third Jeep backed into the fourth, which was trying to move around to follow the second. The man at the fourth Jeep's machine gun fell off, and the third Jeep's gunner fired a burst in the air as he clung to the weapon for balance. The fifth Jeep remained where it was, and the men inside leaped out to return fire.

"Flares!" Cross called over the din.

"Sir!" Lancaster called over the canalphone.

## FOOOSH! FOOOSH!

A second later, a set of magnesium lights lit up the desert night. The flares had been Lancaster's idea. Hidden on the road all along the ambush site and detonated by remote, they blazed to furious life among the startled would-be raiders. At such close quarters, the near light blinded the Malians and made their distant targets nearly impossible to see. From outside the immediate area of effect, the light illuminated the Malians perfectly, making them better targets.

"Fire at will," Cross said quietly.

Thunder shattered the night. Walker shot down the machine gunner on the destroyed lead Jeep. The gunner on the fifth Jeep tried to return fire on Attack One through the magnesium glare. Most of his shots were wide to the left, but Cross heard a few dig into the Growler's rear end. Jannati turned the M134 on him, cutting him down and shredding the vehicle. Those of the Jeep's occupants who'd made it out threw themselves flat, scrambling for cover behind the other vehicles.

Of the two Jeeps that had collided, only one gunner remained in position, and he swivelled his barrel up back toward Attack One. The gunner of the Jeep facing Attack Two opened up, spraying wildly. Some of the bullets tore into Walker's cover, forcing the Chief to dive out of the way cursing in Spanish. Fire from Shepherd's minigun knocked the shooter from the back of the Jeep.

Cross picked off the gunner between the two collided vehicles while Jannati fired on the rearmost of the two Jeeps to keep the gunner who'd fallen off from trying to reclaim his firing position. The gunner retreated toward what minimal cover he could find. Most of the passengers of the two collided Jeeps made it out unharmed, though a burst from Paxton's M4 from Cover Two caught the last one out before he could close the door.

"Frag out!" Williams called as Paxton's man slid to the ground, clinging weakly to the door of the Jeep. The corpsman hurled an M67 fragmentation grenade into the space between the rear bumper and grill of the two collided Jeeps. The blast made the vehicles jump apart and threw a hail of deadly steel fragments into the slavers hiding behind them.

"Suppressing fire," Cross ordered. "Attack Two, move down to flank."

"Sir," Walker replied.

# BANG BANG BANG BANG BANG BANG BANG BANG BANG BANG BANG BANG BANG

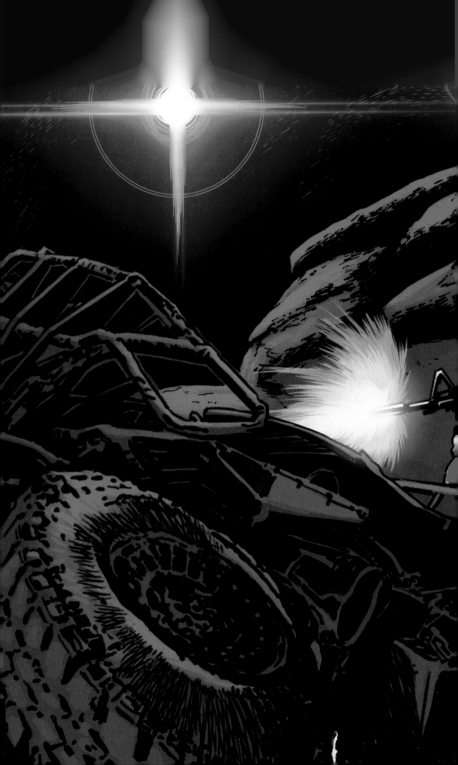

As heavy fire from both miniguns ate away at the savaged Jeeps like starving wolves, Cross and Walker came down to road level from their cover positions at opposite ends of the ambush site. Cross came down behind the disabled ACMAT truck and put it between himself and his men. Walker came down along the inside of the fallen-stone roadblock and took cover behind the first Jeep. The magnesium flares were still burning, but thick smoke from the vehicles and brownish dust from the C4 explosion hung in the air, reducing visibility. Cross lifted his M4 to the ready and began to make his way forward.

"Oh, right, right," Lancaster said in Cross's canalphone, likely at some silent urging from Yamashita. "Sir, you've got . . . it looks like . . . seven left moving down there."

No sooner were the words out of Lancaster's mouth than the passenger door of the half destroyed Jeep nearest Cross fell off. A half-dead Malian lurched out with a bullpup FAMAS rifle clutched under one bleeding arm. His weapon was already trained on Cross as he dropped to one knee to take aim.

# POP!

Yet, Yamashita was faster than them both. The sniper's bullet caught the man in the chest, dropping him at Cross's feet.

"Thanks," Cross said.

"Sir," Yamashita said.

"Make that eight," Lancaster said. "Well, now it's seven."

Cross smirked.

* * *

Between the crossfire and the suppressing fire from the team's attack and cover positions, the remaining men of Bubaga's band didn't stand a chance. Cross understood the grim necessity of the work, but it still sickened him. It was little comfort to think that these men had likely shown no mercy to the people they'd slaughtered or sold into slavery at Bubaga's command.

As for the so-called Spider, they found him laid out by the roadside near an outcropping of rock, a bullet hole in his chest.

"Looks like he was trying to skitter away," Walker said.

"Damage report," Cross said, allowing the bad joke. He was just glad the unpleasantness was over.

"Our Growler's not going anywhere," Jannati said. "The rear end's in a million pieces."

"We'll use the other one to push it onto its Osprey," Cross said. He turned to the team's corpsman. "Kyle?"

"No hits," Williams reported. "One injury. Very minor."

"Injury?" Shepherd said, waving a hand filled with sterile gauze pads. A bright, bloody line had cut his cheek below his left eye. Cross noticed it and cocked an eyebrow, waiting for an explanation. "A chip off the Chief's cover nicked me when they shot it up, Commander."

Cross nodded and turned away. He tapped his canalphone. "Overwatch, report."

"Clear," Yamashita said.

"Clear," Lancaster echoed. "I was about to bring Four-Eyes back here."

"Just land it here and reel in," Cross replied.

"Sir," Lancaster said.

"This was grim, ugly work, team," Cross said to

those assembled before him and over the canalphone. "But well done all the same."

He felt like he should say something else. Maybe something about the villagers they'd protected by what they'd done or something along those lines. But no words seemed to suit the situation. Instead, Cross simply nodded and turned away, switching channels on his canalphone to call the waiting Ospreys. When the call was made, Walker led him aside, looking down the road with a troubled expression.

"What's on your mind, Chief?" Cross asked.

"The base these ones came from," Walker said. "The mine, the cave . . . whatever it is. Bubaga could have more men down there."

"Maybe," Cross said.

"Or slave prisoners," Walker continued. He pointed at the ruined ACMAT. "The look of this truck makes me think he intended to round up the people of Cadran Solaire and bring them there. If he has a place to hold them . . ."

"He could already have other people there," Cross finished for him. "It's a possibility, but it's not the mission. Not our mission, anyway. Our mission's over."

Walker looked down the road, clearly not pleased to hear that.

"Tell you what, Chief," Cross said. "There's a Malian Army base not too far away in Amachach. We'll give them our intel on Bubaga's operation and tell them we got it by working off a tip from Jack Barron. We'll tell them what we did and let them take the credit for it as long as they promise to do two things in return."

"What two things?" Walker asked.

"First, they publicly give credit for the tip to Barron — a tireless Temedt crusader saving lives far from home. Second, they promise to get down here in force and deal with whatever's left in those caves."

Walker frowned. "You think they'll go along with that?" he asked.

"I think Command and I can impress on them the importance of going with the flow on this," Cross said with a smirk.

"I think that would qualify as a happy ending to this mess," the Chief said quietly. He looked up at the sound of distant rotors on the wind. "Ospreys are coming. Off to Amachach, then."

"First to Cadran Solaire," Cross corrected. "Barron needs to know the plan. I'm sure he'll be thrilled to know he's about to be a hero."

"His father too," Walker commented dryly. "Think how proud he'll be of his son, the hero."

"I look forward to reading all about it in the news when he breaks the story back home," Cross said.

"If the Senator plays his cards right, that story could win him the next election," Walker said.

Cross sighed. "So much for a happy ending, Chief."

Walker chuckled. "Sorry, Sir."

# MISSION DEBRIEFING

## OPERATION

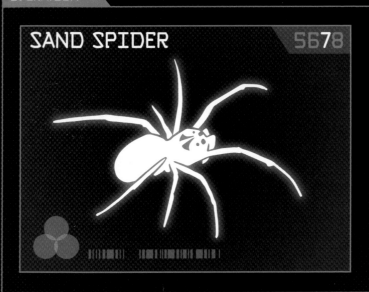

### SAND SPIDER

5678

## PRIMARY OBJECTIVES

- Determine location of hostage

- Escort hostage to safety

## SECONDARY OBJECTIVES

x Avoid conflict with local forces

### STATUS

2/3 COMPLETE

3245.98

# CROSS, RYAN

RANK: Lieutenant Commander
BRANCH: Navy Seal
PSYCH PROFILE: Team leader
of Shadow Squadron. Control
oriented and loyal, Cross insisted
on hand-picking each member of
his squad.

I can't quite say this mission went off as originally planned. But with all things considered, I'm proud of our performance. We demonstrated the ability to think on our feet, and each of you showed you have the composure and adaptability necessary to be a part of Shadow Squadron. And we made Cadran Solaire a safer and better place.

Good job, everyone -- especially you, Lancaster. Welcome to the team.

– Lieutenant Commander Ryan Cross

2019.681

## CREATOR BIO(S)

AUTHOR

# CARL BOWEN

Carl Bowen is a father, husband, and writer living in Lawrenceville, Georgia. He was born in Louisiana, lived briefly in England, and was raised in Georgia where he went to school. He has published a handful of novels, short stories, and comics. For Stone Arch Books, he has retold *20,000 Leagues Under the Sea*, *The Strange Case of Dr. Jekyll and Mr. Hyde*, *The Jungle Book*, *Aladdin and the Magic Lamp*, *Julius Caesar*, and *The Murders in the Rue Morgue*. He is the original author of *BMX Breakthrough* as well as the Shadow Squadron series.

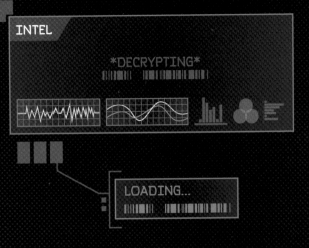

INTEL

*DECRYPTING*

LOADING...

## ARTIST

# WILSON TORTOSA

Wilson "Wunan" Tortosa is a Filipino comic book artist best known for his work on *Tomb Raider* and the American relaunch of *Battle of the Planets* for Top Cow Productions. Wilson attended Philippine Cultural High School, then went on to the University of Santo Tomas where he graduated with a Bachelor's Degree in Fine Arts, majoring in Advertising.

## ARTIST

# BENNY FUENTES

Benny Fuentes lives in Villahermosa, Tabasco, in Mexico, where the temperature is just as hot as the sauce. He studied graphic design in college, but now he works as a full-time illustrator in the comic book and graphic novel industry for companies like Marvel, DC Comics, and Top Cow Productions. He shares his home with two crazy cats, Chelo and Kitty, who act like they own the place.

2019.681

## AUTHOR DEBRIEFING

### CARL BOWEN

**Q/When and why did you decide to become a writer?**

A/I've enjoyed writing ever since I was in elementary school. I wrote as much as I could, hoping to become the next Lloyd Alexander or Stephen King, but I didn't sell my first story until I was in college. It had been a long wait, but the day I saw my story in print was one of the best days of my life.

**Q/What made you decide to write *Shadow Squadron*?**

A/As a kid, my heroes were always brave knights or noble loners who fought because it was their duty, not for fame or glory. I think the special ops soldiers of the US military embody those ideals. Their jobs are difficult and often thankless, so I wanted to show how cool their jobs are and also express my gratitude for our brave warriors.

**Q/What inspires you to write?**

A/My biggest inspiration is my family. My wife's love and support lifts me up when this job seems too hard to keep going. My son is another big inspiration.

He's three years old, and I want him to read my books and feel the same way I did when I read my favourite books as a kid. And if he happens to grow up to become an elite soldier in the US military, that would be pretty awesome, too.

Q/Describe what it was like to write these books.

A/The only military experience I have is a year I spent in the Army ROTC. It gave me a great respect for the military and its soldiers, but I quickly realized I would have made a pretty awful soldier. I recently got to test out a friend's arsenal of firearms, including a combat shotgun, an AR-15 rifle, and a Barrett M82 sniper rifle. We got to blow apart an old fax machine.

Q/What is your favourite book, movie, and game?

A/My favourite book of all time is *Don Quixote*. It's crazy and it makes me laugh. My favourite movie is either *Casablanca* or *Double Indemnity*, old black-and-white movies made before I was born. My favourite game, hands down, is *Skyrim*, in which you play a heroic dragonslayer. But not even *Skyrim* can keep me from writing more *Shadow Squadron* stories, so you won't have to wait long to read more about Ryan Cross and his team. That's a promise.

## INTEL

*DECRYPTING*

5678

### COM CHATTER

-Based on a tip from Agent Bradley Upton, Shadow Squadron sets a trap in Yemen to capture an elusive Iraqi bomb maker nicknamed "The Professor." But the bomb maker escapes, and Lt. Cmdr. Ryan Cross is kidnapped.

Only Shadow Squadron has the talent and technology to stop the bomb maker and rescue the team's leader.

3245.98 ● ● ●

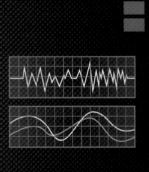

SHADOW SQUADRON

# DARK AGENT

CARL BOWEN

# DARK AGENT

1324.014

*Somewhere in Yemen . . .*

A burst of frigid water splashed into Lieutenant Commander Ryan Cross's face, returning him to consciousness and stealing his breath. He coughed and tried to spit water out of his mouth and nose. His confused mind struggled to fight the fear that he was drowning. Dying.

The terror passed only after he'd gagged and sneezed out the last bit of water. When he opened his eyes, he saw that he had a new reason to fear

for his life. Standing before him was a nightmare from Cross's past. The man held an empty, dripping bucket in his hands.

The man leered at Cross with a twisted mix of delight and hatred. "We've never met." The man spoke in English with an Arabic accent. "And I'd been pleased by that fact. Your reputation precedes you. But now that I have you face-to-face . . . I don't find you all that fearsome."

Cross had to admit that he didn't feel particularly fearsome at that moment. He had been drugged and beaten. His face was a mask of pain, and his left eye was nearly swollen shut. The canalphone he usually wore nestled in his left ear was gone. He still wore the civilian clothes he'd been wearing when he was taken, but his SIG P226 pistol, his utility knife, and his ballistic vest were all gone. It was the loss of the canalphone that troubled him the most. Without it, he couldn't hear or talk to his team.

Cross's first attempt to speak ended in a retching cough, and he spat up one last spray of water.

"You are lost," Cross's captor said. He was a Middle

Eastern man with a scraggly beard and thinning hair. He wore pince-nez glasses, but his dark, beady eyes were visible. The teeth that showed through his sick smile were long and crooked and more yellow than white. Although the face was familiar to Cross, he didn't know the man's real name.

"All the same," the man continued, "a chance at freedom yet remains for you. Perhaps even heroism."

The man stepped back to set aside the bucket. Cross took a look at his surroundings. He was bound to a metal desk chair with plastic zip-ties around both ankles and his left wrist. A nylon rope bound his thighs to the seat. For some reason, his right arm was free.

A glance around revealed that he was in a windowless interior room. A leather couch was opposite him. A wooden coffee table with a glass top was between them. Bookshelves and standing lamps lined one wall. A brown, red, and yellow carpet lay beneath the coffee table.

The man had moved to the threshold of the open door to Cross's right, which Cross noted was the only

way out. "Bring him in," the man said.

Someone outside answered. A moment later, a hunched and hooded figure was shoved into the room. Cross's captor took charge of this second prisoner. The man bound the prisoner's wrists with nylon cord then shut the door behind him. He led the hooded man to the couch and shoved him down. Cross recognized the prisoner's clothing.

"Here lies the gateway to your freedom," their captor said, turning back to Cross. As he spoke, he produced Cross's SIG P226 from beneath his thawb and laid it on the coffee table, close to Cross's side. "You need only raise this gun and shoot this man, and you will be free."

"Or I could shoot you," Cross croaked. "Might be worth it."

"Satisfying to your ego, perhaps," the man said, "but a waste of both our lives. We are not alone here. If your gunshot is not followed immediately by word from me, those who wait outside will come in and kill you both. And you have only one bullet. Enough for him or for me. But I think you will find killing this one rewarding. For if you kill him, not only will I let you live, but I will turn myself in as well. I will submit myself to American justice, whatever form it takes. The only price is this man's life. Will you pay it?"

"Who is he?" Cross asked, trying to stall.

A malevolent smile twisted the man's face. "I should make you decide before I answer that," the man said. "I am not so cruel, however."

He lifted the stiff burlap hood from the prisoner's face. The man beneath was just as bruised and bloody as Cross felt. The left lens of his John Lennon glasses was cracked, and the frame sat crooked on his bleeding nose. He lifted his head, and his eyes met Cross's gaze.

"Ryan," he choked out.

"Agent Upton," Cross said. "Didn't I tell you to stay in the van?"

A weak smile rose to Upton's lips. "I had to pee."

\* \* \*

*One Week Earlier . . .*

Cross rubbed his right forearm as he entered the briefing room of Shadow Squadron's headquarters. The room was already full when Cross arrived. He saw his second-in-command, Chief Petty Officer Alonso Walker hunched over Cross's spot at the head of the conference table. He was operating the computer touchpad recessed into the table's surface. At Walker's command, the globe-and-crossed-swords emblem of Joint Special Operations Command bloomed on the computer whiteboard behind him.

Cross normally set up the briefing equipment before a meeting, but last-minute communications with Command and a painful shot in the arm from the base's doctor had delayed him. Fortunately, Walker had taken the initiative in Cross's absence.

A year ago, Walker's initiative might have agitated the Commander. When he'd left the Navy SEALs to join Shadow Squadron, Cross had received plenty of static from the Chief. Walker had been second-in-command on his previous team. When his superior had been killed in action, Walker had expected to take the lead in his place. Instead, the

brass at JSOC recruited Cross to fill the leadership spot on a new team — Shadow Squadron — with Walker as his second.

It had been a long, hard road breaking the Chief of the habit of trying to subvert Cross's authority. Harder still had been convincing the older soldier that Cross was the better man for the job.

Months of intense training and a long list of successful missions had eventually earned Walker's respect. They'd since forged a bond of brotherhood between them. Cross counted their friendship as one of his greatest accomplishments.

Of course, the successful missions were nothing to dismiss. Shadow Squadron was a top-secret eight-soldier special-missions team assembled from elite soldiers from all branches of the US military. The team included members from the Navy SEALs, Green Berets, Army Rangers, Air Force Combat Control, and Marine Special Operations Regiment. The team travelled all over the world to root out terrorist threats, hunt criminals, rescue hostages, defend foreign leaders, and even fight pirates and slavers.

The US government called on them when they had an interest in military intervention but couldn't act openly for tactical, political, or legal reasons. The the team had succeeded in nearly every mission, which was a major positive listed in Cross's classified service record.

"Morning," Cross said. He began to swipe through icons on the touchpad as Walker ceded the position and took a seat. When Cross tapped the one he wanted, a blank teleconferencing window popped up on the whiteboard. "New mission for us today, and Command says to give it top priority. The CIA's Special Activities Division has identified a high-value Al-Qaeda target operating in Yemen. We're going to go and pick him up."

Cross saw questions rising to his soldiers' lips. Rather than answer them all, he tapped the desk touchpad once more to open the teleconference connection. A familiar face appeared. It belonged to a tanned, smiling white man in his middle-40s, with slicked-back hair, a cleft chin, and sporting John Lennon glasses. The corner of his mouth curled up like he was smirking at the camera. Or at Cross.

"Ryan, good morning!" the man said, as if greeting an old friend after a long absence.

"Agent Upton," Cross replied with a nod. He glanced up at his team to gauge their reactions.

Agent Bradley Upton was a longtime Central Intelligence Agency field operative who worked in secret around the world fighting the war on terror. Working hand-in-glove with the JSOC, Upton helped find the secret places where terrorists armed themselves and executed their plans. His mission was to foil their plans and bring them to justice. His primary centre of operations had been Iraq for many years, but since US forces had largely left that country, Upton had transitioned to Yemen.

The CIA operative did most of his work alone, but he coordinated the efforts of several other divisions. Like Shadow Squadron, those teams performed high-risk black ops. The day Cross had been offered leadership of Shadow Squadron, Upton tried to steal him for his own team. Upton had offered greater glory, more operational freedom, and much more money than the Shadow Squadron position offered. Fortunately, Cross had previously worked with Upton

and knew what kind of man he really was. That was to say, not a good one.

The rest of Shadow Squadron had got to know Upton during their last mission in Iraq. Through favour-trading above Cross's rank, Upton "borrowed" Cross's team for use as bodyguards for an Iraqi CIA informant. The informant had turned out to be a former terrorist who sold information about his former allies in exchange for money, prestige, and political power. He'd also proven himself a coward who'd tried to use his ten-year-old grandson as a sniper shield when assassins had come for him.

The fact that Agent Upton had placed such value on the informant's life earned the team's scorn. Cross understood their hostility toward Upton.

Only one person in the room didn't know Upton as anything other than a name on old files. "And this must be Miss Lancaster," the agent said.

"It's Staff Sergeant Lancaster," Chief Walker said with a scowl.

Staff Sergeant Morgan Lancaster looked to the whiteboard and gave a cool nod. The most recent

addition to Shadow Squadron, Lancaster was one of the first women to enter and graduate from the Air Force Combat Control School. If she took the same offence to Upton's comment that Chief Walker had, she showed no sign of it.

"Staff Sergeant Lancaster," Upton said through an overly sweet smile. "I've read a lot of good things about you. Welcome to the team."

"We're just starting the briefing, Agent Upton," Cross said. "The intel on our target all comes from you. Would you like to do the honours?"

"After you," Upton said. "I'll correct you if you get anything wrong." He smiled again. "Not that I expect you to. You've been very well informed."

Cross didn't like the look of Upton's eyes. Behind his John Lennon specs, Upton seemed distant and calculating. No matter how much he smiled and complimented others, no hint of warmth flickered in those cold eyes.

Cross tapped the touchpad once more. A second window appeared beside Upton's, showing a satellite map of the Arabian Peninsula. Cross highlighted

Yemen, the country on its southwestern corner. In a third window, Cross produced a cropped photo of a man wearing a long gray thawb, a crocheted taqiyah cap, and pince-nez spectacles.

"This is 'The Professor'," Cross said. "One of the most notorious bomb makers in the world."

Cross waited a moment to let that fact sink in. "He has escaped me twice before," Cross said. "And that is not going to happen again."

**\*TRANSMISSION ERROR\***

PLEASE CONTACT YOUR LOCAL LIBRARY OR BOOKSTORE FOR MORE DETAILS...

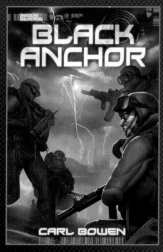

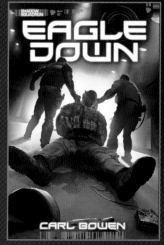

2012.101